MARTIN LUTHER KING, JR.

MARTIN LUTHER KING, JR.

The Story Of A Dream

A Play

By June Behrens   Pictures by Anne Siberell

A Golden Gate Junior Book   Childrens Press   Chicago

To Denise Behrens

Library of Congress Cataloging in Publication Data

Behrens, June.
    Martin Luther King, Jr.: the story of a dream.

    "A Golden Gate junior book."
    SUMMARY: A brief two-act play delineating the efforts
of Dr. King to bring about equal rights for all people.
    1. King, Martin Luther—Juvenile drama. [1. King,
Martin Luther—Drama. 2. Plays] I. Siberell, Anne.
II. Title.
PN6120.A5B366   812′ 5′4   78-23873
ISBN 0-516-08879-3

Photographs courtesy of United Press International

Characters

Martin Luther King, Jr.

Bus Driver

Rosa Parks

Policeman

Miss York

Dina

James

Ida

David

Prologue

Two narrators enter and take their places to the right and left of the curtain.

GIRL NARRATOR: Martin Luther King, Jr. was born in Atlanta, Georgia in 1929. His father and his grandfather were Baptist ministers.

BOY NARRATOR: When he was a boy, Martin went to a school for black children only. There were certain places he and his brother and sister could not go because of the color of their skin. He wondered why.

GIRL NARRATOR: Martin grew up to become a Baptist minister like his father and grandfather. He was called the Reverend Martin Luther King, Jr.

BOY NARRATOR: Many people listened to the powerful words of Martin Luther King, Jr. He said he had a dream—and his dream helped to change the history of our country.

GIRL NARRATOR: Martin Luther King, Jr. lived at a time when there was a need for change. We will see how his dream helped to bring about that change.

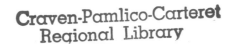

ACT I

Curtain rises

Scene 1: A Classroom. Miss York, the teacher, and four students are discussing the January calendar.

MISS YORK: This month we celebrate the birthday of a great American. His name was Martin Luther King, Jr.

DAVID: Why was he so great?

IDA: What did he do? I've heard his name but I don't know why he was so famous.

MISS YORK: Which one of you can tell us something about Martin Luther King, Jr.?

DINA: My grandmother lives in Montgomery. That's in Alabama. She told me all about him.

MISS YORK: Tell us what she told you, Dina.

DINA: Martin Luther King was a preacher in Montgomery and my grandmother went to his church. She said that a long time ago there was a law in Alabama that black people had to sit in the back of city buses. If a bus was crowded, they had to stand up when white people wanted their seats.

JAMES: Who ever heard of a law like that! Besides, what does it have to do with Martin Luther King?

MISS YORK: James, that law was a bad one and Martin Luther King, Jr. set out to change it. It all started one day when a tired little black lady named Rosa Parks broke that unfair law.

Scene 2: Inside a city bus in Montgomery. Rosa Parks is sitting in a seat near the front. Every bus seat is filled and people are getting on.

BUS DRIVER: All right, folks, let's get up. *(Two black people leave their seats and stand.)* Lady, are you gonna move? *(Rosa Parks remains seated.)* Lady, if you don't give up your seat, I'll have to call that policeman out there.

ROSA PARKS: Go ahead and call him.

BUS DRIVER *(calling through open door)*: Officer! Officer! *(Policeman boards the bus and listens to the driver.)*

POLICEMAN *(to Rosa Parks)*: Lady, if the driver asked you to stand, why didn't you?

ROSA PARKS: Do you think it's right that I should have to stand up for white folks?

POLICEMAN: I don't know, but the law is the law. I'll have to arrest you and take you down to jail for breaking the law.

(Rosa leaves with the policeman as amazed people on the bus talk among themselves.)

Scene 3: *Martin Luther King, Jr. is speaking from a pulpit.*

MARTIN LUTHER KING: This is not a just law and we will protest it. We will not ride the city buses in Montgomery. We will walk. We will ride mules. We will drive wagons and share cars. *But we will not ride a bus until the law is changed! (He pauses.)* "If you will protest courageously, and yet with dignity and Christian love, when the history books are written, in future someone will have to pause and say, 'There lived a great people—a black people—who had the courage to stand up for their rights.' And we're going to do that."

Scene 4: The Classroom.

DAVID: Wow! What happened?

MISS YORK: Martin Luther King and his people did not ride the Montgomery buses for a whole year.

JAMES: Did they change the law?

MISS YORK: Yes, James. The United States Supreme Court decided that people riding on buses could not be separated or segregated because of the color of their skin.

DINA: Then Martin Luther King won a victory for all the people everywhere in the United States, didn't he?

MISS YORK: Yes, and it was the first of many victories, boys and girls. Dr. King became the voice of black people across the land. (*She holds up a poster showing a picture of King.*)

JAMES: Is that all he did, just make it so that people could sit down on buses?

DINA: My grandmother said he marched a lot.

DAVID: What did he march for?

MISS YORK: Martin Luther King was a peaceful man. He did not believe in violence. He thought marching was better than fighting. He led what were called Freedom Walks, or peaceful protest marches. He asked his followers to love their enemies.

IDA: Is that the way he got people to pay attention and listen?

MISS YORK: Yes, Ida. His marches brought bad laws to the attention of people everywhere, including those who made the laws.

DINA: My grandmother remembers when black people could only eat in special restaurants for black people. She couldn't go to movies where white people went.

MISS YORK: That's what the marching was all about, Dina.

JAMES: About eating places and movies?

MISS YORK: James, it was about *giving everyone the same rights.* Was it right to have one set of rules or laws for white people and another set for those with black skin? Remember the bus? Don't you think that all people should be able to sit or stand where they please?

DAVID: But I still don't understand *how* Martin Luther King changed things.

MISS YORK: New laws were needed to bring change, David. Martin Luther King, Jr. marched and preached about the need for change and the right to equal laws and treatment for everyone. Many important people, both black and white, heard his words. They joined the Martin Luther King movement in cities all over America.

IDA: I saw something on TV that happened a long time ago. Marchers were carrying signs and there were so many people you couldn't see the streets or sidewalks.

MISS YORK: Once Dr. King and his friends led two hundred thousand people on a march in the nation's capital, Washington, D.C. It was the biggest public action by a group of people in the history of our country.

(Curtain)

Curtain rises

Scene 1: A park in Washington, D.C. A great number of people are marching and singing.

First Marcher: Brothers, this is a peaceful Freedom March. The people of our country will see us and hear our voices.

18

SECOND MARCHER: They will know that we must have new laws, laws that are the same for all people.

THIRD MARCHER: We will march to the steps of the Lincoln Memorial. That is a good place to talk about equal rights and freedom.

FIRST MARCHER: Let's go!

SECOND MARCHER: Sing out for freedom!

WE SHALL OVERCOME

We shall overcome
We shall overcome
We shall overcome someday.
Oh deep in my heart I do believe
We shall overcome someday.

We'll walk hand in hand
We'll walk hand in hand
We'll walk hand in hand someday.
Oh deep in my heart I do believe
We shall overcome someday.

We shall stand together
We shall stand together
We shall stand together now.
Oh deep in my heart I do believe
We shall overcome someday.

The truth will make us free
The truth will make us free
The truth will make us free someday.
Oh deep in my heart I do believe
We shall overcome someday.

We are not afraid
We are not afraid
We are not afraid today.
Oh deep in my heart I do believe
We shall overcome someday.

Scene 2: Martin Luther King, Jr. is speaking from a podium.

MARTIN LUTHER KING: "Even though we face the difficulties of today and tomorrow, I still have a dream. I have a dream that one day this nation will rise up, live out the true meaning of its creed: *We hold these truths to be self-evident that all men are created equal.*"…

"I have a dream that one day on the red hills of Georgia the sons of former slaves and the sons of former slaveowners will be able to sit down together at the table of brotherhood."…

"I have a dream that my four little children one day will live in a nation where they will not be judged by the color of their skin, but by the content of their character."…

"When we allow freedom to ring from every town and every hamlet we will be able to speed up that day when *all* of God's children will be able to join hands and sing in the words of the old Negro spiritual—*Free at last! Free at last! Great God Almighty, we are free at last!*"

(There is complete silence, then thunderous applause from the crowd.)

Scene 3: In the Classroom. Miss York and the students are busy making Freedom March posters.

24

MISS YORK: Millions of people watched the Freedom March on their TV sets and heard the moving words of Martin Luther King.

DINA: My uncle was there! He carried a sign that said WE WANT TO BE FIRST CLASS CITIZENS. Grandma has a picture of him.

MISS YORK: Americans knew it was time to make new laws. The next year, in 1964, an act called the Civil Rights Act became a law. All people could use parks and stadiums and swimming pools. All restaurants and hotels and movies were open to everyone, black and white alike.

DINA: By then I guess everyone knew how important Martin Luther King, Jr. was, didn't they, Miss York?

MISS YORK: People from around the world knew about him and how he believed in peaceful ways to bring about change. Has anyone ever heard of the Nobel Peace Prize?

JAMES: I've heard about it, but I don't know what it is.

MISS YORK: Each year a prize is given by some citizens of Norway for the promotion of world peace. Prize winners may come from any country in the world. It is a great honor to be named for this prize.

DAVID: I'll bet King won that prize!

IDA: Did he, Miss York?

MISS YORK: Martin Luther King, Jr. was the second black, and the young-

est man ever to receive the Noble Peace Prize. In 1964 he was invited to Norway. The world watched as King Olav V of Norway and many other famous people honored Dr. King. They said that he, more than anyone else, had done the most to promote peace in the world.

DINA: It makes you feel proud, doesn't it!

JAMES: What was the prize? What did he win?

MISS YORK: Dr. King was awarded the Nobel Peace Medal and $54,600.

IDA: That's a lot of money!

DAVID: What did he do with all that money?

MISS YORK: He didn't keep it for himself. He used it to help make his dream of freedom for all come true.

Scene 4: Once more Dr. King is speaking from a podium.

MARTIN LUTHER KING: "Man *can* overcome oppression and violence without resorting to violence."...

"The Nobel Peace Prize was not a personal honor. It is a tribute...to the courage of millions of gallant Negroes and white people of good will."...

"They followed a non-violent course in seeking to establish a reign of justice and a rule of love in the United States."

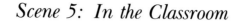

Scene 5: In the Classroom

MISS YORK: Once Martin Luther King and his followers marched fifty-four miles, from Selma to Montgomery, Alabama. It was the year after the Civil Rights Act of 1964 opened public places to all people.

JAMES: What were they marching for this time?

MISS YORK: Dr. King wanted everyone to know that voting laws needed changing. After that march the Voting Rights Act of 1965 was passed. It did away with tests and taxes which had stopped many black citizens from voting.

IDA: I guess lots of people loved Martin Luther King, didn't they, Miss York?

MISS YORK: He had many followers, but many people did not think as he did. There were those who wanted to fight and to stop him from making changes in the laws.

DINA: You mean, they wanted to hurt him?

MISS YORK: In 1968 Martin Luther King went to Memphis, Tennessee to help the garbage workers. He and some friends were standing on the balcony at his motel. Suddenly the echo of a shot was heard and Martin Luther King slumped to the floor.

JAMES: What happened?

DAVID: Somebody shot him!

MISS YORK: Martin Luther King, Jr. was killed by an assassin. A man filled with hate took the life of a man who preached love.

IDA: What a terrible thing to happen to such a good man!

IDA: MISS YORK: People around the world wept and mourned the death of Martin Luther King, Jr. He died a young man, but his spirit and accomplishments live on today. In his thirty-nine years of life Martin Luther King changed America's thinking about the human rights of all people.

(Curtain)

The story of a remarkable man who, in the 1960's, changed the face of the United States of America for all time, is told in the form of a play, a play to be acted out or to provide boys and girls with a rich reading experience. Here is a graphic picture of Martin Luther King, Jr. and his accomplishments, presented in a new and unforgettable way. Who King was, what his goals were, how he went about realizing his dream of equality for all people regardless of the color of their skin, are told in terms children will readily understand and appreciate. In a series of short scenes, shifting from a typical classroom situation where a group of today's students are discussing King's birthday anniversary, to vignettes of the high points in King's career—the famous bus boycott in Montgomery, the Freedom March to Washington's Lincoln Memorial, the winning of the Nobel Peace Prize—events are highlighted with excerpts from King's actual speeches as the story of this unique American unfolds. The book is enhanced by the sensitive illustrations in stunning full color by Anne Siberell.

JUNE BEHRENS spent many months researching the material for her play about Martin Luther King, Jr. In it she has brought to bear her knowledge and perception, born of long experience, of what children best understand and empathize with. A reading specialist in one of California's largest public school systems since 1965, Mrs. Behrens holds a Credential in Early Childhood Education and has a rich background of teaching experience at all elementary grade levels. She is the author of a score of books for young readers, including two former plays, *Feast Of Thanksgiving* and *The Christmas Magic-Wagon,* published by Childrens Press. When she is not teaching and writing, she and her husband, a well-known educator, spend vacations travelling to various parts of the world. They make their home in Redondo Beach, California.

ANNE SIBERELL, in addition to being a talented book illustrator, is a distinguished fine arts painter as well as a woodcut and etching artist. Her work has been widely exhibited in museums and art galleries throughout the country and she has won a number of awards for her print-making and graphics. She is the illustrator of two former Childrens Press titles, *Feast of Thanksgiving* and *Who Found America?* She has also written and illustrated a book of her own, *Houses,* published by Holt, Rinehart and Winston. A native Californian, Mrs. Siberell received her art training at UCLA and Chouinard Art Institute in Los Angeles. She now lives in Hillsborough, a suburb of San Francisco, with her husband and three sons.